Leisure Arts 36

Chinese
Flower Painting

Jane Evans

SEARCH PRESS

Introduction

The pictures in this book were all painted with Chinese brushes using oriental ink and colours on unsized *shuan* paper.

The possibilities offered by the special properties of the brushes and the paper, together with the particular qualities of the ink and colours, provide a marvellously versatile and expressive medium for the spontaneous portrayal of a subject.

There are many styles of Chinese Brush Painting. The pictures here were done using a freestyle *Wen Jen Pai* method. As few strokes as possible are used to create the effect and each stroke is done with confidence and speed to give life and vigour to the subjects.

Taoist philosophy teaches that all things have a *chi*, or nature, which governs the way they are and how they act. When I paint a flower, I am not trying to produce a botanically accurate representation, rather I am trying to capture the flower's innate spirit. In order to be able to be true to this spirit, it is of course vital to understand how plants are constructed and grow and how they react to sun, wind and rain. My eyes are therefore as important as my brush. I do not have a flower in front of me when I paint because I am not trying to portray an individual specimen. Rather, I study flowers in their natural settings and then return to my studio to try to capture their nature on paper.

In keeping with this philosophy, I follow the Chinese Brush Painting tradition of starting a picture with the most important thing in it. If the painting is of a rose branch, then the roses come first and the leaves and stem later. It is the flowers that are the most obvious expression of the plant's nature. The wash is put on last of all.

The feeling which someone looking at a Chinese Brush Painting should have – that the flower has been caught at a moment in time – is helped if the picture can be completed 'in one breath'. To do this, I try, wherever possible, to add the last stroke before the first one has dried. Clearly, this is not feasible for more complicated pictures and for a few techniques it is not desirable, but the principle of working as fast as possible holds true for most freestyle painting. I prefer to make the mistakes occasioned by speed and to attempt a subject several times until I achieve the effect I seek, rather than to go more slowly and lose the spontaneity of the medium. In any case, the nature of the paper and the brushes means that working slowly only produces flat and lifeless results.

Taoist philosophy also teaches the importance of space, and this, combined with the Buddhist admiration for simplicity, has influenced the aesthetics of Chinese painting. Pictures are seldom cluttered; indeed the spaces in a painting are an important element of its composition.

Flowers have traditionally been a major subject in Chinese Brush Painting. In the past, flower pictures were regarded as more important than those of animals, birds, or even people. Students learning under a traditional Chinese Brush Painting master today still begin with flowers and plants and concentrate on these for some time before moving on to other subjects. Many flowers have traditional meanings in China, some of them attributed by Confucius: plum blossom is an emblem of winter and symbolizes long life and purity; the orchid stands for love, beauty and fertility; the chrysanthemum symbolizes autumn and also cheerfulness; the peony represents spring and is also thought to symbolize love and female beauty. The lotus is a symbol of summer and fecundity. It was thought of as sacred and is the emblem of one of the Immortals in the Taoist pantheon.

I enjoy painting flowers because they offer ample opportunity for exploiting the artistic potential of the medium. They also provide an exciting challenge because those very virtues of Chinese Brush Painting which contribute so much to the liveliness of the pictures – the holding capacity and versatility of the brush, the absorbency of the paper and the permanence of the colours – require good technique if they are not to become drawbacks rather than advantages. Once you have mastered this technique, you will appreciate the unique character of a successful painting done 'with a Chinese brush'.

If you follow the instructions in this book you will be able to adapt the methods and paint many other flowers. I have used the techniques described to paint the cyclamen on this page.

Materials

Chinese brushes and paper are essential for this medium and Chinese ink and colours desirable if you want to achieve spontaneous vigour and subtle colours in your paintings.

Brushes

Whereas a watercolour brush has its bristles first clamped into the haft and then trimmed, the bristles of a Chinese brush are carefully shaped and stuck together to form the head, which is then glued into the handle. The brush will hold a very large amount of ink or paint, allowing you to do all the petals of a flower, or several leaves, with one brush load. It can be loaded with several colours at once to create a variegated effect. Alternatively, just the tip of even a large brush will draw a fine line. By using differing pressures of the brush and by varying the angle of the head in relation to the paper, the painter can call on a large repertoire of expressive strokes. The bristles can also be twisted or split to give a number of interesting effects.

Brushes for Chinese Brush Painting come in three main types according to the hair they are made from: soft brushes are usually white and are made from goat, sheep or rabbit hair; resilient brushes are usually labelled as 'wolf' or 'fox' hair but are more commonly made from weasel or sable; coarse brushes are normally made of horsehair.

When painting flowers I use a resilient brush if I want to achieve a tidy edge to petals and leaves, and when I want the brush to keep its shape for several strokes. Resilient brushes are also the best kind for 'feathered' and 'split' brush strokes. I use horsehair brushes for textured strokes and to achieve the tattier effects. I use a soft goat hair brush if I want a blurry outline.

For each subject in this book I describe the particular brush I use. If you do not have exactly the right brush you should try to use one which is as like it as possible and remember that it will make a difference to the size and shape of your strokes. Washes, which are added after the subject of the painting is completed, I do with a 3 cm (1½ in) hake brush.

Once a painting is completed I back it with paper to stretch and strengthen it and for this I use a 3 cm (1½ in) bristle mounting brush. This can be bought from a supplier of Chinese Brush Painting equipment, or you can use a bristle art brush of the correct width.

Whenever possible I try to buy the best brush available in the size and type I want. Price is a good guide to quality in most Chinese Brush Painting equipment and it is not worth trying to economise, especially with brushes. Achieving the right effect with a poor quality brush demands much better technique than achieving it with a good one. It is better to buy a few good brushes than several cheap ones.

Ink and colours

I use both Chinese and Japanese ink and colours. Although you can buy bottled ink, I prefer to grind my own for three reasons: firstly, the act of grinding helps to loosen my shoulder and relax me ready for painting; secondly, I can grind the ink to the consistency I want – the bottled ink can be too liquid for some purposes; and thirdly, and perhaps most importantly, the preservative that is added to the bottled ink undermines its fixing property and it may run when a wash is put on it. I use a Chinese or Japanese ink stick. Basically this consists of soot and glue shaped into an oblong and decorated with characters and a picture. I grind the ink on a slate inkstone.

Most Chinese and Japanese colours are translucent like watercolours. A few, usually greens and some blues, have had white added to make them opaque. All of them are permanent once they have bonded with the paper and dried, so that I can add washes on top of images. Chinese painting colours are made of plant or mineral extracts. Traditionally, the mineral colours come as powders which have to be mixed with glue before use. The vegetable colours come as small chips of solid colour which need melting together into a block with hot water. It is also possible to buy already prepared colours: Chinese painting colours are sold in tubes and Japanese paints come in dishes of solid colour. Occasionally I use gouache colours which have similar fixing qualities, but I prefer the translucence and the colours available in the traditional Eastern paints. As with the brushes, I describe the colours I use for each subject. Naturally you can choose any colour schemes you like – flowers come in an inifinite variety of shades.

Paper

My paintings are usually done on unsized *shuan* paper. This is very absorbent and the colour binds with the paper. The nature of the paper makes a wide range of effects possible. Clean, crisp strokes can be done provided they are executed swiftly. By working more slowly, on the other hand, a gentler, slightly furry image can be achieved. At first beginners may find the paper difficult to use but, once they master its properties, they will find that what at first appear to be disadvantages can be exploited in ways which offer new and exciting artistic dimensions. Amongst other things, the absorbency of the paper provides endless possibilities for creating interesting wash effects.

There are many different sorts of Chinese and Japanese paper on the market now. Most widely available is machine-made paper, sometimes called 'moon palace' paper, which is sold in rolls of varying width. This has some sizing but not enough to prevent its feeling like blotting paper to people unaccustomed to it. I have not used it for any of the pictures in this book but they could all have been done on it. It is relatively cheap and easy to come by and, with the proviso that it does not take washes very well, it makes a reasonable substitute for *shuan* paper if this is not available. The consistency of the sizing varies from roll to roll. The smoother side is the less absorbent one.

Shuan paper, which can be made from bamboo fibre, is also fairly reasonably priced, if not so widely available as machine-made paper. It is hand-made and comes in individual sheets or in rolls of ten sheets. Quality and consistency can vary according to the type of *shuan* and it is always worth experimenting with a new batch to discover its virtues and faults. Although all *shuan* is absorbent, it does not all absorb in the same way and some varieties are better natured than others. A good *shuan* can be very adaptable and is surprisingly strong for something that looks so flimsy.

Other essentials

I work at a table that is high enough to allow me to stand to wield my brush freely from the shoulder. I only sit to paint small details. I cover the table with Chinese painting felt which is off-white, but any dull colour would do. When I apply a wash I place a blanket under the painting.

My palette is a white ceramic fondue plate which has a number of sections. I find this more useful than the traditional Chinese flower-shaped palette, because the bigger sections allow me to load a large brush with several colours more easily. It is also ideal for mixing enough colour for a wash.

I have paperweights to keep my paper flat while I am painting and I always have several jars of clean water and a roll of kitchen paper to hand as well.

Learning about the materials

If you are unfamiliar with the paper, brushes and ink, it is a good idea to play with the materials a bit and learn something about their properties, before you try any of the flower subjects in this book. Get used to the absorbency of the paper and discover the versatility of the ink, and particularly of the brush, before you tackle the first subject which is plum blossom.

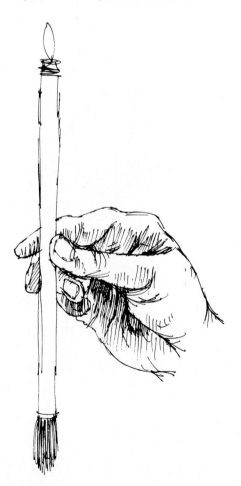

The illustration on this page shows how the brush is held. It must be clasped loosely between the thumb and the middle finger. The index finger should be at the front with the middle finger but it is only there for guidance, not grip. The ring and little finger are at the back with the thumb and help to move the brush fluidly. Only if the brush is held in this way can it be controlled properly, so that you can deploy the full range of strokes of which it is capable.

For free vigorous strokes, the brush is held quite high up the haft, with the wrist steady and the brush wielded from the shoulder. For small details it is easier to hold the brush nearer to the bristles but it should still move freely from the shoulder, not the wrist. Even though to begin with it will seem to make the strokes more difficult to execute, it is essential to persevere with the correct grip until it becomes second nature.

Before you can get to know the brush and paper you will need to grind some ink. To do this, transfer a few brushfuls of water on to the ink stone. Grind the stick in the water on the stone with a firm circular motion until you have thick, very black, ink. You can then transfer some of the black ink on to your palette and dilute it with water to create all shades of grey.

The best brush to begin with is the one you are going to need to paint plum blossom flowers. It is a resilient brush which has bristles 1.5 cm (¾ in) long and about 0.5 cm (¼ in) in diameter. If the brush is a new one you will need first to wash off the sizing which holds the bristles together. Do this thoroughly with water. Then begin by just filling the brush with grey ink and discovering what a large amount it will hold. Do a stroke on the paper and find out how far a brushful will take you.

Practise using the brush at different angles. In this book, I talk about using the brush 'along' its bristles and 'across' its bristles. The three illustrations at the top of the page opposite show what I mean by this, (a, b, c). To use the brush along its bristles, you usually pull it in the direction the bristles 'grow', (just occasionally you may push it to achieve a rough stroke). To use the brush

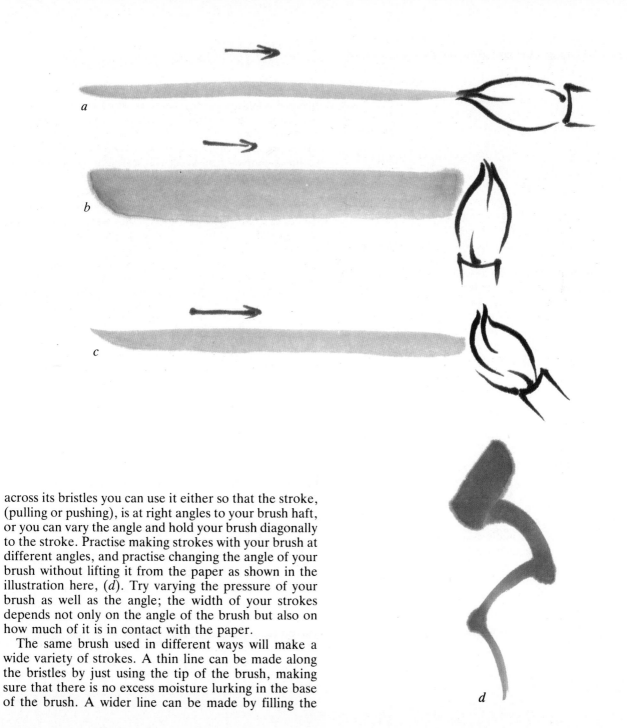

across its bristles you can use it either so that the stroke, (pulling or pushing), is at right angles to your brush haft, or you can vary the angle and hold your brush diagonally to the stroke. Practise making strokes with your brush at different angles, and practise changing the angle of your brush without lifting it from the paper as shown in the illustration here, (*d*). Try varying the pressure of your brush as well as the angle; the width of your strokes depends not only on the angle of the brush but also on how much of it is in contact with the paper.

The same brush used in different ways will make a wide variety of strokes. A thin line can be made along the bristles by just using the tip of the brush, making sure that there is no excess moisture lurking in the base of the brush. A wider line can be made by filling the whole brush with ink and using it across its bristles. You can make a split line by 'feathering' the end of the brush; in other words by spreading out the bristles at the tip.

Because of its holding properties, a Chinese brush can be loaded with several tones at once to achieve a variegated effect without sacrificing liveliness by having to work at blending the colours with several strokes.

The full effects of Chinese Brush Painting are the result of the interaction between the brush, the ink and colours, and the paper. You will by now already know how absorbent the paper is. You need to learn how to control that absorbency and turn it to your advantage. A stroke made quickly will have clean edges, and a stroke made slowly will have a furry edge.

Because of its absorbency, the paper will tend to blunt strokes. During the book I talk about both blunt and tapered strokes. If you stop a stroke on the paper it will have a blunt end. To taper a stroke you have to continue the brush stroke into the air. This is the same whether the brush is used along or across its bristles.

There is another characteristic of the paper that is worth knowing about before you start plum blossom. Because the paint is absorbed into the paper, the first stroke is the one that remains the most prominent. However many strokes are put over the first one, they will always sink behind it. This characteristic of the paper is evident even when the first thing added to it is clean water and it is the chief reason why mistakes in Chinese Brush Painting cannot be corrected.

When you have begun to feel comfortable with your paper, ink and brush, you can go on to the flowers. Traditionally, Chinese Brush Painting is learnt by mastering a sequence of subjects. Each subject is an end in itself – you are for example striving to paint a beautiful plum blossom, and it is also teaching you skills you will need for the next subject. Try therefore to follow the sequence of the book and practise each subject thoroughly before moving on to the next. The Chinese believe that only when you have learnt to do something correctly will you begin to understand why you should do it the way you were taught. This book cannot be a complete course in Chinese Brush painting, but it is designed to give you a good grounding in one important aspect of it. How thorough that grounding is largely depends on you.

Mounting

Once a painting is completed I add my 'signature' in the form of a Chinese 'chop' or seal. Whether I add one or two chops and where I place them on the picture is determined by the composition of a particular painting. My chops were designed for me by my teacher but some Chinese shops in the West will translate names into seal script and make chops to order.

Finished paintings need to be stretched and strengthened by mounting them on a backing sheet. This can be heavy *shuan* paper, good quality watercolour paper, heavyweight wallpaper lining paper, or lightweight board, although the last is difficult to use on larger paintings. I make sure that my backing sheet is at least two inches larger all round than the picture.

To mount a picture I lay it face down on a clean, wipeable table. I use wheat-based wallpaper paste, preferably a brand recommended for lightweight papers, which I mix so that it has a loose 'dropping' consistency. I apply the paste to the back of the painting with a mounting brush. I work out gently from the centre of the picture, applying a little glue at a time, and easing out air bubbles and creases as I go. The painting should flatten and 'stick' to the table.

I place the centre of my backing sheet on to the centre of the painting and press it carefully down, smoothing it out firmly from the centre to eliminate air bubbles. I peel the backing, with the painting now stuck to it, off the table. If there are any air bubbles or creases, these can be gently eased out from the front with a dry wash brush.

I trim off all but 1 cm (½ in) of the excess backing paper and lay the painting flat to dry. I put paper weights round the remaining margin. Once the picture has completely dried, I trim this off too.

The painting is now ready for framing. It can be put in a conventional Western frame, either with a normal matting mount, or with a traditional Chinese silk surround. There are places in the West which can do silk mounting. Traditionally, Chinese paintings are not framed but are mounted on scrolls for hanging.

Plum blossom

Do-it-yourself books on Western art typically provide step-by-step illustrations, which begin with a sketch and progress through washes and blocking-in colour to the fine detail which is added at the end. Freestyle Chinese Brush Painting is not done like this: there is no preliminary sketch; the wash is usually the last thing added, and details are often put on with the same stroke as the shape or, at least, as you go along. Instead of step-by-step illustrations, therefore, I have tried to break the paintings down into their elements. These elements are presented here in the order in which they were done in the paintings.

When I paint I do not begin with a sheet of paper which is the size the finished painting is going to be. I begin with a much larger piece and, if I am working with a roll of *shuan*, I do not cut the roll until after the picture is finished. I prefer to let my brush determine the size of my painting and the subject dictate the amount of space the composition requires. For this reason I have not started each description of a painting with its size, as is customary, because this is the last thing I decide upon. While doing the paintings for this book I have necessarily been constrained to some extent by the square format but there is no need for you to be. Chinese Brush Paintings are seldom square.

A traditional Chinese Brush Painting course begins with the student learning how to paint plum blossom. This is probably because plum blossom teaches many of the basic skills needed for brush painting. It teaches control of the depth of ink tone and of the consistency of the ink. It teaches control of the amount of moisture on the brush. It uses different brush angles and pressures. It requires blunt and tapered strokes. It begins to teach simple loading of the brush with different tones. For this reason, it is worth spending some time practising plum blossom so that you master these basic techniques.

Plum blossom is the exception to the rule about starting with the flowers. I begin the painting of plum blossom, with the branch. The finished painting can be seen on page 11. Because the flowers are rather small in relation to the branch it is the latter which determines the composition. I grind some ink and dilute some of it with water on my palette to make a dark shade of grey.

Fig 1

To do the branch in Fig 1 I use a resilient brush that has bristles 3 cm (1½ in) long with a diameter of 1 cm (½ in). A brush this size is known as a 'bamboo' brush.

I fill the whole of the brush with the grey ink and wipe off the excess liquid on the side of my palette, which I always do after filling my brush. I then dip the tip of the brush in the thick black ink on the ink stone. Beginning at the top, and using the brush across its bristles with the tip of the brush towards the darker side of the branch, I press the full length of the brush head on to the paper while simultaneously moving it in the direction the branch is growing. As I move along the branch I change the pressure of my brush and the angle of the head, without either stopping or taking the brush off the paper. I keep the brush moving fairly fast and try to keep in my mind the shape of the branch that I am trying to create.

Having done the main branch with a single stroke, I add the smaller branches. I taper most of the small side branches but make a few of them blunt. (I've added arrows to the figure to show which way my brush was moving). The gaps that appear in the branch as the ink begins to run out are called 'flying white' and add texture. If there is more flying white than there is ink this means that the brush is too dry; none at all may mean that the brush is too wet. A very blurred soggy branch is either the result of too much moisture on the brush, or of working too slowly. Occasionally I leave a space between sections of branch to allow for blossom since this cannot be added on top of the ink. The black splodges of thick ink are put on while the grey is still damp so that they blend in slightly. They are meant to represent lichen or moss.

I use a resilient 'plum blossom' brush for the flowers. I dip the brush in water and then lightly dry it with a kitchen towel. I dip the very tip of the brush into Chinese bright red. Holding the brush as upright as possible, I place the tip on to the paper and, keeping this in the same spot, I roll the heel of the brush (which just contains water) around it to make a petal shape. The effect of the water in the heel of the brush is to create a two-tone effect because the red bleeds into it as the stroke is made.

A single flower is built up as shown in Fig 2. Not all the petals are seen whole; for those where only the top is showing I simply lay my brush down sideways and pull it

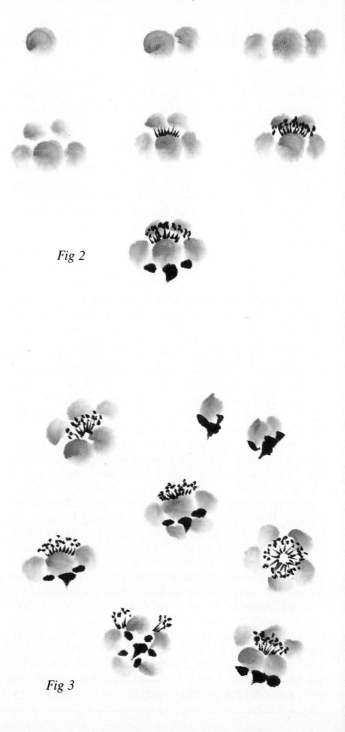

Fig 2

Fig 3

slightly giving it a curve as I do so. I try to do a single flower without redipping my brush between petals. The stamens should be added before the petals have dried. I use the tip of my brush and make an odd number of stamens with quick, short, tapered strokes along the brush. The pollen is added with random dabs of the tip of my brush, again using very black ink. For the sepals I fill my brush about halfway down with black ink. I place the filled section of the brush sideways to the petals and press down. For the sepals on either side I then lift the brush cleanly off the paper. For the centre sepal I press down in the same way but then I pull the brush across its bristles and do a very short tapered stroke. As with the stamens, the sepals should be done before the petals are dry. Fig 3 shows some different blossom shapes.

For the bee in Fig 4 I use the tip of my 'plum blossom' brush to draw the head, thorax and stripes in black. The body is made by laying the brush, filled with yellow and tipped with vermillion, with its tip towards the head. I add the antennae, with blunt strokes, and the legs, tapering the feet. The legs grow from the thorax. I make the shape of the wings with dark grey ink using a light 'feathered' stroke, beginning at the thorax and tapering the end. I make the front pair of wings slightly bigger than the back one. With my brush filled with watery white, I lay it over the wings with the tip towards the thorax. Last of all I add a few touches of dark grey to the tips of the wings.

Fig 4

The finished painting

Orchid

The Chinese talk of the 'four friends' of plant painting. These are plum blossom, orchid, chrysanthemum and bamboo. Students of Chinese Brush Painting learn these four plants before any others. Between them they provide a varied repertoire of techniques and strokes.

To paint an orchid plant, such as the one in the finished painting on page 15, I begin with the flowers. Westerners sometimes find this a somewhat strange way to start, but it fits in with the philosophy of beginning with the main element of the picture. The flowers are

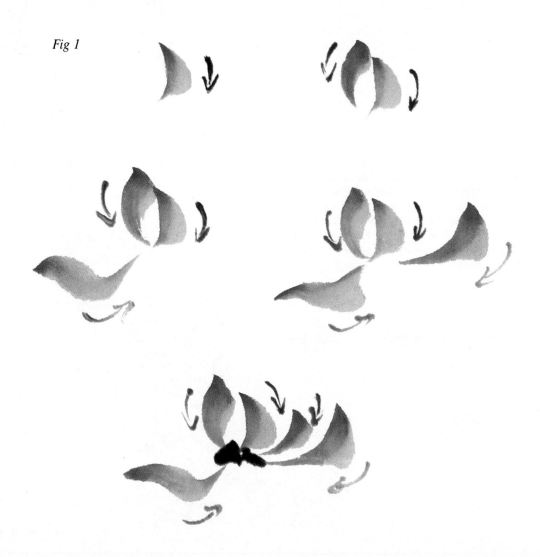

Fig 1

what give this plant its identity and they are therefore the point from which I begin.

I use a resilient 'orchid' brush which has bristles 1.5 cm (¾ in) long with a diameter of approximately 0.5 cm (¼ in). I load the brush with Chinese green and tip it with Japanese peony purple. I begin with the two central petals and do them with the bristles at a slight angle. The purple tip forms the top of the petal and I gradually increase the amount of the brush that is in contact with the paper to make the shape of the petal. I turn the brush so that I am working along the bristles and taper the stroke for the base of the petal. The stroke for each of the two larger outer petals is essentially the same but this time I slightly turn the brush as I press it down, so varying the angle of the bristles, and I taper the stroke with the brush at a slight angle, rather than along its head. The fifth petal is done in much the same way as the first two petals, trying to keep it slightly smaller than they are.

As with plum blossom in the previous demonstration, I try to do a whole flower with a single brushload. Sometimes it is necessary to retip the brush with purple if this runs out. The stamens are added with very black ink. These consist basically of three quick dabs with the brush which are all done in one movement without completely lifting the brush in between each dab. Fig 1 shows the building up of an orchid flower.

When adding stalks to flowers, it is very much easier to begin at the flower. The stalk is done along the bristles, alternately pausing and moving quickly while varying the direction, all the time working freely from the shoulder. I keep the individual segments of stem fairly short because this helps them to stay lively. Fig 2 shows a small section of orchid stem.

Fig 2

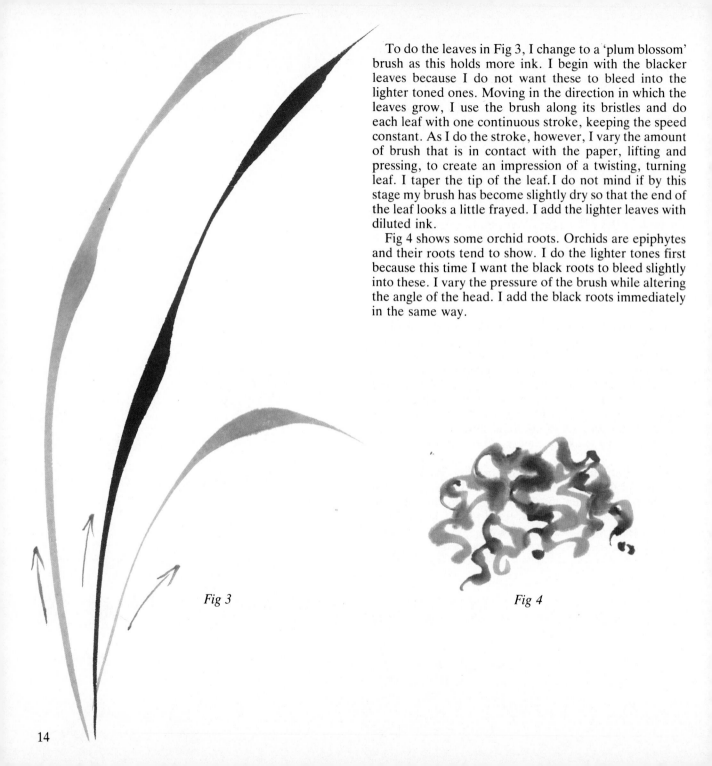

To do the leaves in Fig 3, I change to a 'plum blossom' brush as this holds more ink. I begin with the blacker leaves because I do not want these to bleed into the lighter toned ones. Moving in the direction in which the leaves grow, I use the brush along its bristles and do each leaf with one continuous stroke, keeping the speed constant. As I do the stroke, however, I vary the amount of brush that is in contact with the paper, lifting and pressing, to create an impression of a twisting, turning leaf. I taper the tip of the leaf. I do not mind if by this stage my brush has become slightly dry so that the end of the leaf looks a little frayed. I add the lighter leaves with diluted ink.

Fig 4 shows some orchid roots. Orchids are epiphytes and their roots tend to show. I do the lighter tones first because this time I want the black roots to bleed slightly into these. I vary the pressure of the brush while altering the angle of the head. I add the black roots immediately in the same way.

Fig 3

Fig 4

The finished painting

15

Chrysanthemum and bamboo

It may seem odd to the Western reader to find bamboo included in a book about flower painting but it is impossible to discuss the basics of Chinese Brush Painting without reference to bamboo. Not only has bamboo always been an important theme, but it involves the use of techniques which are fundamental to a great deal of Chinese Brush Painting. Bamboo also lends itself to compositions with different flowers – for example it seemed to me to be the ideal way to set off the chrysanthemums in the finished painting on page 19.

However, I begin the painting with the flowers. I fill the tip of a 'plum blossom' brush with thick orange taken straight from the dish. I place a mark for the centre of the flower in Fig 1 and, beginning in the centre and without pausing mid-stroke, I do each of the five petals that form the middle of the flower – out and in. Having done these five petals, I decide which way I want the flower to face. I then fill in the rest of the petals by working round the flower, making those on one side of it longer and foreshortening others to give the flower head an angle. For the flower seen from the side, I put the sepals in first. For each sepal I place the brush so that its tip will form the top of a sepal and press down quickly, lifting the brush cleanly off.

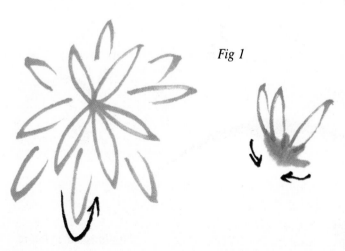

Fig 1

The method for the stem in Fig 2 is very similar to that used for plum blossom branches (*see pages 9 and 10*). I work from the flowers and increase the thickness of the lower part of the stem by having more of the brush in contact with the paper and by increasing the angle of the head. I add some emphasis with black ink.

To do the leaves in Fig 3, I change to a 'bamboo' brush. I begin the leaf in Fig 3a with the central segment. Starting from the top where the leaf is turned over, I lay the full length of the brush sideways on to the paper. I pull it down at right angles, turning it very slightly to give the leaf a curve, and continue the stroke into the air. I do the two side segments in the same way, making them rather shorter than the central one.

I do the central section at the top of the leaf in Fig 3b first. I lay my brush on the paper with its tip towards the centre of the leaf and with its bristles going in the same direction as the vein. I press down firmly with the whole of the brush and pause. I lift the brush cleanly off the paper. The remaining four sections of leaf are done in exactly the same way but with the brush at an angle to the vein. I do the two sections at the base of the leaf first leaving a gap for the remaining sections. I make this rather narrower than the stroke will be because I want some overlap.

The veins are added in very black ink with the brush tip. I do these while the grey is still damp and use tapered strokes starting from the centre and moving outwards. The veins should be firm and lively.

Fig 3c shows a small leaf similar to those which tend to grow near the flower head. This time, I begin with the brush tip towards the top of the leaf and do a stroke very similar to that used for an orchid petal (*see page 12*).

Fig 4 shows bamboo stems. To do these I use (not unexpectedly) a 'bamboo' brush. I fill the whole of the head with grey ink and then pick up a little undiluted ink from the stone with the tip of the brush. To make each segment I press the full length of the bristles on to the paper, pause very briefly, and then move the brush in the direction the bamboo grows with the bristles at a right angle. At the end of the segment I press down lightly and pause again. For the top segment I taper the

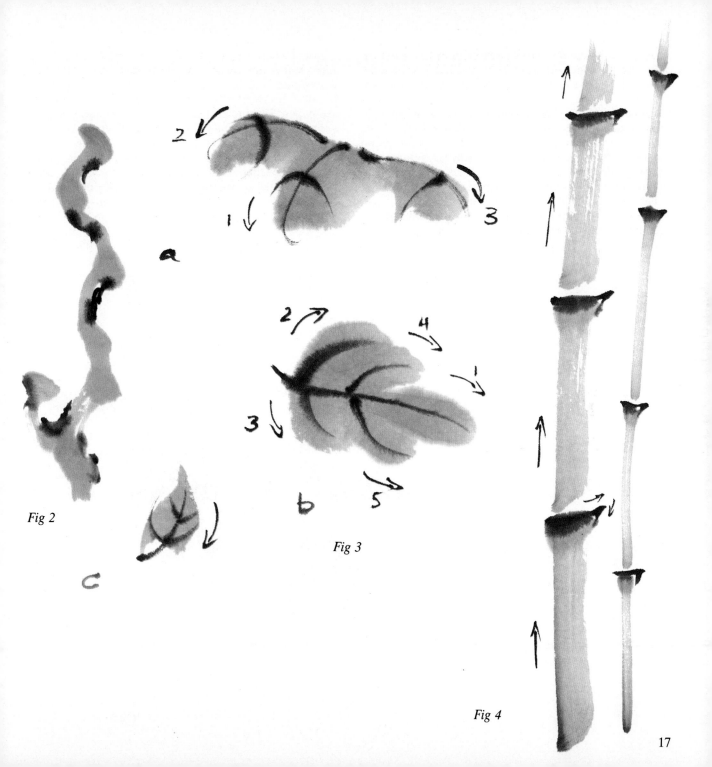

Fig 2

a

b

Fig 3

c

Fig 4

17

stroke into the air instead of pressing down. Each stem of bamboo is done with a single brush load. I want some 'flying white' for texture and I work fast to give my stem vigour.

For the narrower stem I load my brush with grey and gently touch its sides into black. I do the strokes along the bristles, pausing and pressing at the beginning and end of each segment in the same way as before, and tapering the top section. I use thick black ink to emphasise the joints while the stems are still damp.

The smaller bamboo branches such as those in Fig 5 always grow out of a joint. I do them with the brush tip, keeping the individual segments short and tapering the last section.

For the leaves in Fig 6 I fill my brush with black ink. Each leaf is done with a single fluid stroke which both begins and ends in the air. The word stroke is very apt because this is exactly what I do: I stroke my brush on to the paper. Starting at the base of the leaf and beginning with my brush in the air, I bring it down on to the paper, working along the bristles and increasing the pressure until the whole brush head is in contact with the paper. Without pausing, I immediately start to lift the brush again, gradually tapering the stroke to form the tip of the leaf. I do not mind if the tip of my leaf splits slightly as leaves do tend to fray.

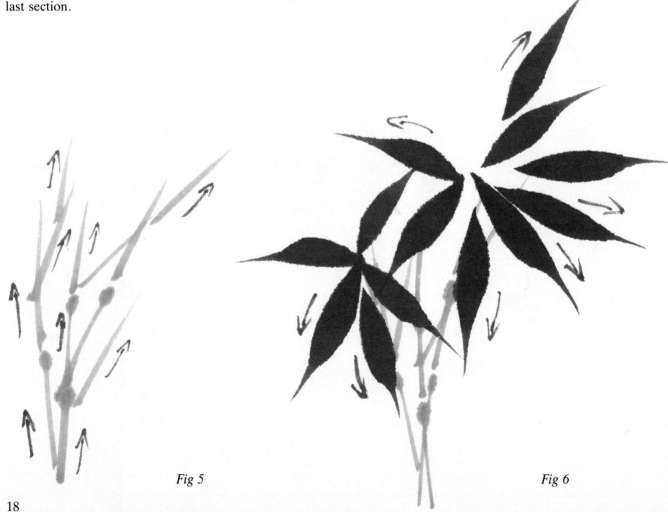

Fig 5

Fig 6

The finished painting

Peony

For the peony flower in the finished painting on page 23, I use a large horsehair brush 4 cm (1¾ in) long with a diameter of 1 cm (½ in). I fill it with Chinese white and tip it with peony purple. With another brush, I paint round the base of the bristles with purple.

Fig 1a shows how the flower is built up. I begin with the large petal in the centre of the flower and place the brush so that its tip will form the bottom of the petal. I lay the full length of the brush on the paper and press down. Keeping the tip of the brush in the same place, I roll the base of the bristles round, pressing and lifting to make a variegated petal. The technique for the other petals is basically the same. Most of these are somewhat smaller and for some there is no need to have a purple tip to the brush, since they are partially hidden behind other petals. By using a horsehair brush with stiff bristles, I can achieve a ragged edge to my petals. When positioning the petals I try to leave a gap in the middle of the flower for the seed pod. Once the petals are all done, I run some very watery yellow into the base of each one. This helps to give the flower depth.

I add a seed pod in the space left, similar to the one in Fig 1b. This is made up of segments rather like a cantaloupe melon, although only the top of it shows above the petals. I fill a 'plum blossom' brush with a mixture of Chinese green, indigo and a touch of burnt sienna and make the segments. I add a little more indigo and burnt sienna to the colour and accentuate the divides in the seed pod. I wash and dry my brush and use it to blend the light and dark tones together. I highlight the segments with Chinese green mixed with gouache white and blend this in, I add the stamens with thick, white gouache, using blunt strokes. The pollen is dabbed on with a mixture of vermillion, red and yellow splodges.

Fig 1a

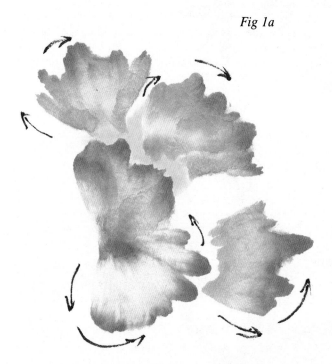

Fig 1b

Fig 2 shows a peony stem. For the section nearest the flower, I use a 'plum blossom' brush filled with a mixture of yellow, indigo, burnt sienna and a hint of red. I spread the tip of the brush out so that it will give a stroke of even width and touch the sides of the brush into red. I begin at the flower and do a clean stroke along the bristles. I add the side stems with the tip of the brush. I refill my brush with the same colour mixture, tip it with red, and do the sepals where the stalk joins the flower, using the same stroke as for the chrysanthemum leaves and orchid petals (*see pages 17 and 12 respectively*). I add a touch of black to the tip of these and a splodge or two of green.

I change to a 'bamboo' brush for the woodier part of the stem. The method is essentially the same as for a chrysanthemum stem (*see page 17*) except that, instead of using grey ink, I use a dilute mixture of green, yellow, burnt sienna and indigo. I add the black highlights immediately and some splodges of green for lichen. The orange tendrils are done with a flick of the tip of the brush in the manner of the smallest orchid petals.

For the leaf in Fig 3 I use a very large horsehair brush, 6 cm (2½ in) long with a diameter of 1.5 cm (¾ in), for the maximum tatty effect. I fill the brush with a colour mixture similar to that I used for the branch and tip it with ink. I begin with the central section and position the brush with its tip towards the base of the leaf. I lay the brush on the paper and pull it along its bristles, turning the brush head as it moves until it is at right angles. Then, without altering the speed of the stroke, I lift the brush off into the air. I add the two side sections of leaves in the same way but without increasing the angle of the brush head as much. The method for all the leaves is basically the same. I try to vary the colour slightly and I change the shapes too. I add the veins with thick black ink while the leaf is still damp. I try not to be too tidy with these. I add splodges of green for lichen.

Fig 2

Fig 3

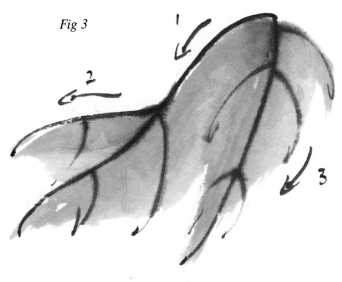

21

To do the butterfly in Fig 4c I use a 'bamboo' brush. I fill it with yellow and then dip the top half of the bristles into vermillion. I begin at the outside of the top right hand wing and lay the full length of the brush at the outer edge and pull it towards where the body will be, lifting it slightly so that the wing narrows (*see Fig 4a*). Without taking the brush off the paper or altering the angle of the head, I pull it backwards and roll it round, in the manner of a plum blossom petal, to form the lower right hand wing, finishing with the brush on the body side of the wing. Still without taking the brush off the paper, I pull the tip across and roll the brush again to make the second lower wing, once again bringing my brush in towards the body. I then pull it up and outwards, along its bristles, to form the final wing, just pressing down slightly at the wing tip.

I add some splodges of red to the tips of the wings. I use a 'plum blossom' brush for the body with a mixture of Chinese green, indigo and burnt sienna (*see Fig 4b*). I add darker markings and highlight the spaces in between as I did for the seed pod on the previous page, adding

the head, thorax, legs, antennae and wing markings with black ink, using the tip of a small horsehair brush (*see Fig 4c*).

This painting has a simple tea wash. I lay it face down on an old blanket or thick piece of felt and damp it evenly all over with my wash brush. The 'wash' on the finished painting consists of six bags of Assam tea to about a mugful of water. The tea is made normally and well stewed. I fill my wash brush very sparingly with the tea and start brushing it on to the painting, using light, firm, even strokes. I vary the direction of the strokes and spread the brush load of tea as far as it will go and as evenly as possible. I then refill the brush, again sparingly, and repeat the process, making sure that I begin to apply the new tea in an area of paper that already has some wash on it. If wet spots start to appear where the paper is sticking to the blanket, I very carefully lift the paper and mop underneath to prevent these marking the painting.

Fig 4c

Fig 4a

Fig 4b

The finished painting

Iris

This is a painting of a clump of flag irises with a dragonfly. I begin with the brightly coloured flowers. For the open flower I take the same large horsehair brush that I used for the peony petals and fill it with yellow, adding vermillion to the top third of the bristles. I start with the central large petal, laying the full length of the brush with its tip downwards, towards the centre of the outside edge of the petal. Keeping the heel of the brush in the same place so that it forms the body of the petal, I swing the brush round to make one half of the petal. I repeat the stroke for the other half, without reloading my brush. I then do the other two large petals with a stroke similar to that used for larger orchid petals, (see page 12). The size of the brush governs the size of the stroke.

The three vermillion petals at the top of the flower are done next, this time using a stroke similar to the one used for the smaller orchid petals. The upstanding, small yellow petals are added in the manner of the orange tendrils on the peony (*see page 21*). I do the base of the flower by laying the brush on the paper with its tip towards where the stem will be. While the petals are still wet, I add the stripy markings in dark red, with the tip of a small horsehair brush or the split end of a dry resilient one. I do the petals of the half-opened flowers and buds before their sepals. Once I have done all the bright flowers and buds, I fill the same brush with a mixture of yellow, burnt sienna and indigo and add the sepals – using a stroke similar to that used for a peony sepal and the stalks.

For the leaves I add more indigo to the colour mixture I used for the stalks. With the same brush as for the flowers, I do them as if they were a combination of orchid and bamboo leaves. I keep them straighter than orchid leaves, with fewer pressure alterations, and I stroke the paper in much the same way as for bamboo (*see pages 14 and 18 respectively*). I add turned-over leaf tops where it seems appropriate. I put on the clearly defined leaves after the bright flowers.

Next I do the dragonfly. I use a 'plum blossom' brush filled with vermillion and begin with the head and thorax. I add the body in Chinese green, beginning at the thorax and using a stop-start stroke similar to the

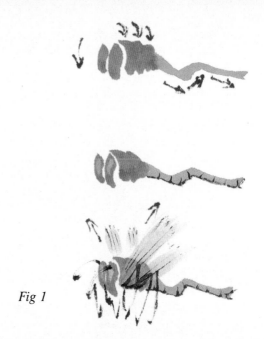

Fig 1

one used for a small side branch. I highlight the eyes with white and add black markings to the body. I put in the antennae and legs and add the proboscis. The markings on the wings are then added in the same way as for the bee (*see page 11*) and the watery white put over these for the shape, although, this time, I pull the tip along the bristles away from the thorax for length, before pressing the heel down to make the fatter part of the wing. I add markings to the wing tips.

For the paler flowers, buds and leaves I first damp the paper all over as if for a wash, although I keep it face-up. I then do them in exactly the same way as the clearer ones using fairly dilute colours. Because they are being put on after the others they will sink behind them.

I leave the painting to dry before turning it over and redamping it for the wash. The wash method is exactly the same as for the peony (*see page 22*), except that I use a dilute mixture of yellow, burnt sienna and indigo instead of tea, and I try to concentrate the wash behind the irises. I begin where I want the darkest colour to be and work carefully outwards. I do not add any colour round the outside of the painting but I am very careful to brush the colour from the centre evenly outwards as far as it wants to go so that the colour fades away imperceptibly.

The finished painting

Lotus

I begin the painting of the lotus with the flower. I fill the same horsehair brush that I used for the peony and the iris with Chinese white and tip it with bright red. I lay the brush with the tip towards the top of the first petal (to the left of the flower centre) and press down firmly with the heel, while turning the brush so that the tip moves round to form the outer edge of the petal, as I did for the iris on page 24. I do this twice to form the two sides of the top of the petal. I then turn the brush so that the tip is now towards the base of the petal and lay it down again, pressing so that the white on the heel bleeds into that left by the previous strokes. Where only the top of the petal will be showing, I omit the third stroke. For the petals that are hanging down, I find it easier to begin with the single stroke to make sure the petal grows out of the flower in the right place. If I want a petal to have a turned over portion, I do this first. A few of the outer petals are done in the same way as the two large, side petals of the iris. I leave a space for the seed pod in the flower centre. I run a very dilute yellow wash over the inside surfaces of the petals and add the red markings with a very dry brush. The petals of the bud are done in the same way, although I try to keep these slightly neater.

The centre of the flower is added in the space provided and shows a portion of the seed pod. The method is exactly the same as for the peony (*see page 20*) although the shape is different and I add markings to the top for the seed holes. The stamens and pollen are also the same as for the peony. The stalk is done in the same way as a peony stalk. It is wider than these because it is done with a bigger brush and the colour is Chinese green, toned down with a touch of indigo and burnt sienna. The black whiskers are added while the stalk is wet and I am careful not to be too tidy with these.

I make copious quantities of black ink and even more diluted grey ink for the leaves. I fill the horsehair brush that I used for the peony leaves with grey. Using the brush across its bristles, I do a series of strokes, working out from the centre, to form about two thirds of the bulk of the first leaf. I refill my brush with grey and tip it with black. I lay the brush on the paper so that the tip forms the outer edge of the leaf and the heel overlaps the area

already painted. I roll the brush round as I did for the peony petal, lifting and pressing to create the ragged edge of the leaf. I do not mind if gaps occur as lotus leaves tend to be holey, but I do redip my brush in mid-leaf if it runs out of ink and I retip it if all the black gets used up. Where a leaf is turned-over, I do the section that looks nearer first. I add the veins while the leaf is still wet. I add a colour wash to the leaf, blending orangey brown on the outer edges with a mixture of sky blue, indigo and burnt sienna from the centre.

The wash is done before the grass is added. I damp the paper with my wash brush but keep the painting face up to make it easier to see where I want the colour variations to come. The basic wash colour on this painting is a mixture of sky blue, indigo and burnt sienna. I vary the proportions slightly for different areas of the painting. The technique is exactly the same as before but, instead of leaving the paler areas round the edge as I did for the iris, I leave lighter areas in the picture itself. Because I want a wet effect, as if it is raining, I apply some slightly darker toned mixture with brush strokes that all go in the same direction – downwards – instead of blending it as usual by changing the direction of the strokes. I concentrate these areas particularly below the leaves.

While the paper is still damp and using the brush I used for the flowers, I add the grass. I do this as if it was bamboo with rather long stalk segments and elongated leaves. I add some Chinese green splodges.

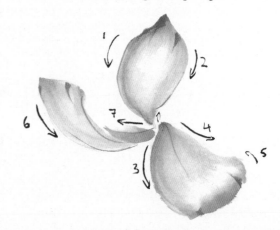

The finished painting

Rose

To do a rose flower like the ones opposite I use a large goat hair brush which has bristles 4 cm (1¾ in) long with a diameter of 1 cm (½ in). I load it as I did for the plum blossom – the heel of the brush contains clean water and just the top third of the bristles is dipped in the colour – in this case dark red taken straight from the pot. The two-tone effect is created by the red bleeding into the wet area made by the heel of the brush.

I start with the two central petals and, working in the direction of the arrows, I taper the stroke down on to the paper along the bristles. Keeping the pace steady, I gradually alter the angle so that I am working across the bristles, with the tip describing the inside edge of the petal. As I do this, I increase the pressure with the heel so that it forms the paler area. I gradually turn the brush again and taper the stroke off the paper along the bristles. I emphasise the outside of the petals gently. I add the rest of the petals in the same way, *making them gradually larger as I work outwards.*

I draw the shapes of the buds in the finished picture with firm, bold strokes, using a mixture of dark red, burnt sienna and indigo. The tops of the buds are done with a bamboo leaf stroke but using only the tip of the brush. To fill in the petal areas, I tip my clean brush with red and lay it – once for each gap – so that the heel damps the wide part while the red on the tip bleeds into it.

The stem is the same colour as the bud, and the thorns are added in black by laying the tip of the brush at right angles to the stem and pulling it away, tapering the stroke across the bristles.

The rose leaves are done in varying tones of grey ink, with the same large soft brush. I try to do each leaf in one movement, using a stroke like that used for sepals. I begin at the base of the leaf and press down with the whole of the brush head before tapering the stroke to form the tip. Occasionally, I may do a leaf in two halves. I add the veins in black.

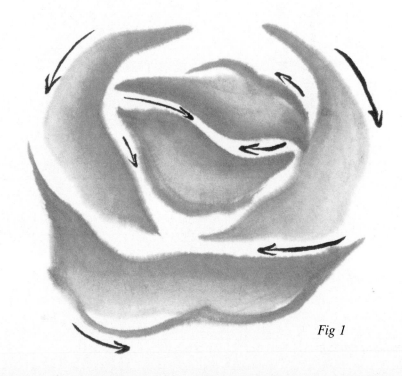

Fig 1

The finished painting

Wisteria

For the wisteria flowers I use a 'plum blossom' brush loaded with Japanese squab red and tipped in peony purple. To do a single flower I lay the full length of the brush on the paper and, working in towards the centre of the flower, I do a scooping stroke with the bristles at right angles. I do a second petal coming in to meet the first one, as shown in Fig 1a. I redip the brush in peony purple and do the two small petals by laying the brush on the paper at the appropriate angle and pressing down, lifting the brush quickly and cleanly off, as shown in Fig 1b. I fill my brush with very dilute yellow and put a light wash into the gap between the petals. I arrange a group of flowers in a cluster and build it up. Towards the bottom of the cluster I add some buds which are done with the same stroke as the smaller petals. I add the stalks in a mixture of burnt sienna and indigo.

Wisteria leaves tend to grow in fan-shaped groups above the flower clusters. I use a 'bamboo' brush and begin by putting in the main vein. I load the brush with Japanese light green, toned down with touches of yellow and burnt sienna, and tip it with peony purple. The individual sections are done in exactly the same way as

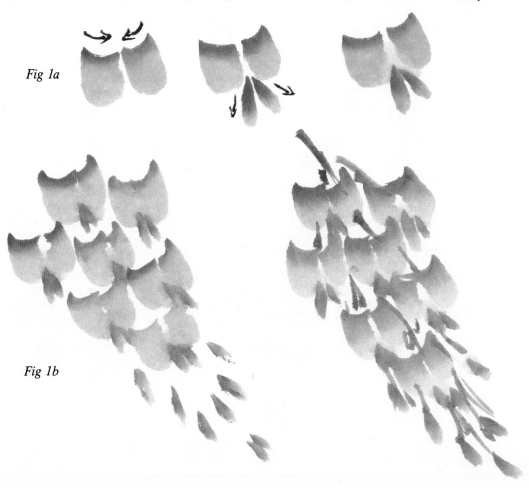

Fig 1a

Fig 1b

The finished painting

the sections of chrysanthemum leaf. I place the tip of the brush towards the vein and press down quickly and firmly, once for each leaf. Occasionally, I retip the brush with purple although I like to have some variations from leaf to leaf. I add the smaller veins.

The vine of the wisteria is done by the same basic technique as plum blossom branches and chrysanthemum stems but I exaggerate the twists and bends. I add the black highlights and the splodges of Chinese green lichen while it is still wet. The tendrils are done with free fluent strokes of the brush tip.

When I add the wash to the painting, I want to create the impression that the viewer is on a wisteria-hung balcony, somewhere in the Mediterranean, early in the morning when the light is very soft. I damp the paper evenly all over with my wash brush, keeping the picture face-up. I put the sun on in gouache white tinged with yellow. With a clean brush, I blend the edges into the surrounding damp paper.

Leaving that to dry slightly, I then put in a line for the horizon with a mixture of indigo and sky blue, using a 'bamboo' brush and then blending the line into the paper with a clean wash brush. The basic colour for the rest of the wash is a mixture of sky blue, a small amount of indigo and a touch of squab red. The technique is exactly the same as before. I blend light and dark areas, concentrating the latter behind the flowers and round the edges and bottom of the sea area. I make the sky very slightly lighter than the sea, and I make sure that there is a light area round the sun and on the water beneath it. I add a little yellow tone to these areas. I add ripple marks on the water, using my 'bamboo' brush. I do a wavy, dark line and then highlight one side of this with Chinese white. I blend these ripples in with a clean wash brush. Last of all I add a hint of more flowers and leaves, using watery colour.

The author would like to thank DKE for the illustration of the correct way to hold a brush, and Mev for his help and suggestions. She also sends her appreciation to those of her students who lost lesson time while she was working on the paintings in this book.

First published in Great Britain 1990
Search Press Limited,
Wellwood, North Farm Road,
Tunbridge Wells,
Kent TN2 3DR

Copyright © 1990 Jane Evans

U.S. Artists Materials Trade Distributors:
Winsor & Newton, Inc.
11, Constitution Avenue, P.O. Box 1396, Piscataway, NJ 0885–1396

Canadian Distributors:
Anthes Universal Limited
341 Heart Lake Road South, Brampton, Ontario L6W 3K8

Australian Distributors:
Jasco Pty Limited
937–941 Victoria Road, West Ryde, N.S.W. 2114

New Zealand Distributors:
Caldwell Wholesale Limited
Wellington and Auckland

ISBN 0 85532 638 7

Publisher's Note

There is a reference to "wolf" hair and other animal hair brushes in this book. The publisher's enquiries show this is a very grey area. Importers are unclear whether these brushes are made from wolf, sable, weasel or some other animal fur.

It is the publisher's custom to recommend synthetic materials as substitutes for animal products wherever possible. At the time of publishing, there is no known wholly satisfactory alternative for animal hair in Chinese brushes. Precedent in general supports that alternative materials may eventually be found for this purpose.